What Other Church Marquees Have Said

Compiled by
Dr. Alton E. Loveless

Copyright 2015
By
Dr. Alton E. Loveless

ISBN 978-1-940609-36-2

This book was printed in the United States of America.

To order additional copies of this book contact:

FWB Publications
Enchanted Acres
1006 Rayme Drive
Columbus, Ohio 43207
Alton.loveless@prodigy.net
Dr. Alton Loveless, Owner

FWB

For years I have collected and written the saying and quotes I have found on church signs and from time to time took photos of churches and their signs.

Likewise I enjoy old tombstone sayings, especially the funny ones.

Thank you for your interest.

--Alton Loveless

Table of Contents

Quotes For Your Bulletins Or Marquees

1 cross + 3 nails = 4 given

1,189 chapters! – The Bible.

2 things you can count on: death and taxes. Are you ready for both?

2009 years ago heaven touched earth the rest is 'his story'

24 hour lifeguard on duty - see john 3:16

3 nails + 1 cross = 4 given

3 nails 1 cross 4 given

50 shades of grace

7 days without prayer makes 1 weak

A

A – B – C always believe Christ.

A baby's life is God's choice

A baby is God's opinion that life should go on

A bad attitude is like a flat tire. You won't go anywhere until you change it.

A bad attitude spoils the gift

A bad day at work is better than a good day in hell.

A Bible falling apart belongs to someone who isn't!

A Bible that is falling apart, usually reveals a life that isn't

A candle loses nothing by lighting another candle.

A child of the king should bear a family resemblance

A church is a gift from God...assembly required

A clean conscience makes a soft pillow.

A closed mouth gathers no foot

A cloudy day is no match for a sunny disposition!

A cold church is like cold butter, it doesn't spread well.

A cup of wisdom is worth far more than a vat of knowledge.

A day has been well spent when you included God in all you did.

A day hymned in prayer, is less likely to come unraveled.

A diamond is a piece of coal that stuck to its job.

A diamond is coal that survived the pressure

A family altar can alter a family

A father is someone you can look up to no matter how tall you get.

A fellow who says it can't be done is likely to be interrupted by someone doing it.

A fire is hot. The sun is hotter. Hell will be the hottest

A fool with a tool is still a fool.

A foul mouth is evident of a polluted soul

A gift is not a gift until given.

A gloomy person brightens a room by leaving it.

A good mother is worth hundreds of schoolmasters.

A good pill to swallow is your pride.

A good place for the 'buck to stop' is at the collection plate.

A good tree cannot bear bad fruit, and a bad tree cannot bear good fruit....thus, by their fruit you will know them.

A goose never voted for an early Christmas

A grateful mind is a great mind.

A grudge is a heavy thing to carry

A half-truth is a whole lie

A happy man marries the girl he loves

A hug: the ideal gift. One size fits all!

A humble mind is the soil from which thanksgiving springs.

A large heart can be filled with small things

A lot of kneeling will keep you in good standing.

A man can stand a lot as long as he can stand himself.

A man is not ready to live if he is not ready to die.

A man is rich according to what he is, not what he has.

A man is rich according to what he is, not what he has.

A man leaves his father and mother and is united to his wife, and the two become one flesh.

A man loves his sweetheart the most; his wife the best, but his mother the longest

A man wrapped up in himself makes for a small package

A man's character is like a fence. It cannot be strengthened by whitewash.

A merry heart doeth good like medicine.

A mind always employed is always happy. This is the true secret, the grand recipe, for felicity.

A mind fixed on God has no room for evil thoughts.

A mother is the heart that God gives to every family.

A mother understands what a child does not say.

A mother's love is the fuel that enables a normal human being to do the impossible.

A mother's love is as close as it gets to God's love

A parent's life is a child's guidebook

A parent's life is a child's instruction manual

A peaceful heart finds joy in all of life's simple pleasures.

A person committed to God provides the best model for us

A person is never as empty as when he is full of self.

A person who hungers for money will starve to death spiritually!

A person without prayer is like a tree without roots.

A praying man does not sin – a sinning man does not pray

A problem not worth praying about isn't worth worrying about.

A promise made to another is a promise made to God

A radical is someone with both feet planted firmly in the air.

A sensible thanksgiving for mercies received is a mighty prayer in the spirit of God. It prevails with him unspeakably.

A ship in harbor is safe – but that is not what ships are for

A sin is anything which separates you from God and/or your neighbor.

A smile is a light in the window of your soul.

A smile looks good on everyone!

A stranger is a friend you've never met

A successful marriage isn't finding the right person... it's being the right person.

A temper is like a fire. If you let it get out of control, it can cause a lot of destruction.

A thankful heart is not only the greatest virtue, but the parent of all the other virtues

A truly rich man is one whose children run into his arms when his hands are empty.

A wise child hears his father's instruction.

A wise son makes a glad father.

A word of love can make a world of difference

A workless faith is a worthless faith.

A world of love makes a world of difference.

A wrong train of thought can lead to a wrong station in life.

A. S. A. P. – always say a prayer!

Accept Jesus Christ, or prepare to take the heat

Accept miracles.

Act your praise, not your shoe size.

Action without thought is like shooting without aim.

Adam and eve picked the apple – Jesus picked you for his harvest

Admitting mistakes is not a fault, failing to correct is.

Advent – the season of preparation to give and receive; joy, love, hope, and peace

After a good dinner one can forgive anybody, even one's own relatives.

Alive is better, Jesus lives

All atheist will believe 1 day!

All Christians have the same boss.

All men die, not all men live!

All my life I've always wanted to be somebody. But I see now i should have been more specific.

All sinners not welcome since we only have room for 350.

All who come in as sinners, go out as winners!

Always remember that hell is un-cool.

America bless God

An eternity without God will be hell.

And who do you say He is?

Any man can be a father but it takes someone special to be a dad.

Anyone can count the seeds in an apple. Only God can count the apples in a seed.

Anything over your head is under God's feet

Aonvatlis- let God unscramble your life.

Are these genes in your jeans or are you just happy to see me?

Are we giving the kind of love we seek from God?

Are you lost? Get found with GPS...God's plan of salvation.

Are you ready????

Are you trading heaven for hell?

Around the corner, around the world

Art doesn't transform. It just plain forms. As long as you are the message, you can never be the messenger.

As long as you are the message, you can never be the messenger.

As one door closes, another opens.

As the same sun that melts clay so God's revelation of himself softens the hearts of some and hardens the hearts of others

Aspire to inspire before you expire

At the end of your rope? Look up

Atheism is a non-prophet organization no prophets no profit

Atheist? Better pray you're right.

ATM inside...atonement, truth and mercy

Attempt to get a new car for your spouse - it'll be a great trade.

Attend the church of your choice... seating available here

Attitudes are contagious. Is yours worth catching?

B

B u s y-buried under Satan's yolk

B-basic i-information b-before l-leaving e-earth

Be "hearers" first, then "doers" of the word

Be a fountain, not a drain.

Be an organ donor...give your heart to Jesus

Be careful how you live. You may be the only Bible some people read.

Be ye fishers of men. You catch em, and He'll clean em

Beat the Christmas rush, come to church this Sunday!

Become a prepper, prepare for Christ coming back.

Belief in God will not earn you a spot in heaven. Obedience will.

Believe to receive

Better to face the truth now, than after death

Beware of the high cost of low living!

Biblical preaching is always in season

Big bang theory, you've got to be kidding ... God

Blessed are the flexible, for they shall not get bent out of shape!

Blessed is he who trusts in the lord

Body piercing saved my life

Bowling alley: please be quiet. We need to hear a pin drop.

Brush your mind with the word of God,

But guilty and forgiven

C

Cafeteria: shoes are required to eat in the cafeteria. (Socks can eat any place they want.)

Call 911...this church is on fire

Can you spell love? Jesus can.

Can't sleep? Try counting your blessings

Can't sleep??? Don't count sheep... talk to the shepherd!!!

Can't sleep?

Car dealership: the best way to get back on your feet — miss a car payment.

Challenges in life can make you either bitter or better.

Change how you see, not how you look.

Character is doing the right thing, even when you don't feel like it.

Character is doing what's right when no one is looking.

Character is how you treat those who can do nothing for you.

Children an heritage of the lord

Children brought up in church are seldom brought up in court

Choice, not chance, determines destiny.

Christ believed, his salvation received

Christ is our steering wheel, not our spare tire

Christ takes us as we are and makes us what we ought to be

Christ's return is near, don't miss it for the world

Christian see, Christian hear, Christian do!!!

Christians are not perfect and innocent,

Christians have a lifetime guarantee.

Christians, keep the faith... But not from others!

Church is a hospital for sinners...not a museum for saints

C'mon over and bring the kids ... God

Cold comfort: being as good as the next guy

Come as you are you are not too bad to come in and you are not too good to stay out.

Come early for a good back seat

Come in and leave your sins at the cross

Come in and try our supper. It is free and can free you.

Come on in- God has been expecting you!

Come on in- God is still expecting you!

Come to church – don't wait for the hearse to bring you.

Coming soon: manufacturers recall. Are you ready???

Contentment - enjoying the scenery on a detour

Could God nominate you for best actor?

Count your blessings, not your problems.

Count your blessings, not your troubles

Courage is fear that has said its prayers!

D

Daily devotion is better than yearly resolution

Danger! God at work

Dear God, i have a problem. It's me.

Death and taxes. Are you ready for both?

Death: the end of excuses, the beginning of eternity

Devil riding your back? Take off the saddle!

Discipline is doing something you dislike

Do not bring with you the memories of the past. Let them serve as your guide to keep moving on your journey. Happy New Year!

Do not regret growing older. Many are denied the privilege.

Do not wait for the hearse to take you to church

Do the math. Count your blessings!

Do you have any idea where you are going ... God?

Do you have any idea where you're going?

Do you keep your Bible as close as your cell phone?

Doing right is never wrong.

Don't be a link in a chain of rumors.

Don't be fooled-come hear the truth

Don't come here alone, bring a friend.

Don't confuse what can't be done with what hasn't been done.

Don't confuse what can't be done with what hasn't been done.

Don't count on luck, trust in the lord

Don't forget about your soul

Don't get caught with your spiritual alarm off!

Don't give up. Moses was a basket case, too.

Don't hide your light, come shine with us!

Don't let others bad choices, steal your joy in Christ

Don't let six strong men carry you to church

Don't let the littleness in others bring out the littleness in you

Don't let the noise of the world drown out the peace of God's love.

Don't let worry kill you. Let the church help

Don't make God a priority in your life. Make him your life!

Don't stand nose to nose, stand shoulder to shoulder

Don't tell God how big your problems are. Tell your problems how big your God is!

Don't tell God how big your storm is, tell the storm how big your God is

Don't use your 'freedom' as a rationale for sinning.

Don't wait for 6 strong men to carry you to church

Don't wait for the hearse to take you to church

Don't wait for things to settle down to start going to church just settle down and go.

Done

Don't be a day late and a prayer short to enter his kingdom

Don't count sheep. Talk to the Shepherd

Don't gamble with your soul

Don't let a dark past cloud a bright future,

Don't make me come down there ... God

Down on my knees i learned how to stand.

Drought got you down? Living water here

Dusty Bibles lead to dirty lives

E

E V I L- Live spelled backwards

Earthly works die with us. God's work lives immortal

Enjoy this day! Compliments of God

Enlighten up!

Eternity is a long time to think about what you should have

Eternity is timeless

Eternity somewhere...the choice is yours, for now!

Eternity....smoking or non-smoking?

Every member was once a guest...come join us!

Every saint has a past– every sinner has a future!

Every day is a gift, that's why they call it the present.

Everyone welcome except the devil

Evil triumphs when good men do nothing.

Evolution is no solution

Exercise daily. Walk with God. Run from sin.

Exposure to the son may prevent burning

Exposure to the son, will prevent you from burning later

F

F E A R- false evidence appearing real

Failure is success if we learn from it.

Faith in action raises your spiritual temperature

Faith in Jesus can turn stumbling blocks into stepping stones

Faith is responsibility...our response to God's ability.

Faith makes things possible, not easy.

Faith sames alone – But faith is never alone.

Faith takes God at his word, whatever he says.

Faith: no proof required / doubt: no proof enough

FEAR—face everything and rise

Feeling gratitude and not expressing it is like wrapping a present and not giving it.

Feeling like no one cares? Give us a chance to prove you wrong.

Fight truth decay...study the Bible daily

Fill your years with life, not your life with years.

Filling station

Firefighters can rescue you, but only Jesus saves.

Five minutes after you die you'll know how you should have lived

Follow me ... God

For all you do...his blood's for you

For every goliath there is a stone

For every sin the devil has an excuse.

Forbidden fruit creates many jams

Forecast...the son will shine forever!

Forgive someone today, before it's too late.

Forgive your enemies, it messes with their heads.

Forgiveness is not automatic

Free soul wash today!

Free trip to heaven...details inside

Freedom is not free.

Freedom is not free....Jesus paid the price for your freedom...freedom from sin!

Freedom is nothing but a chance to be better.

Freedom is the oxygen of the soul.

Fresh word served every Sunday

Fret and worry are caused by calculating without God.

Friends don't let friends die without Jesus

Frog... Fully rely on God!

Fully rely on God! Are you a frog?

G

Gamboling losses are a volunteered tax on stupidity.

Gardening for God brings peas of mind

Get rid of your pride, before you have to swallow it.

Get right or get left

Give all your worries and cares to God.

Give thanks for each day...you'll never get to live it over again

Glory to God in the highest heaven

Go to church, don't wait for the hearse to take you

Go...Teach...Baptize

God answers knee-mail

God believes in you

God can do anything, but fail.

God can make all things new, even you

God can turn your biggest mountain into a grain of sand

God cares about you

God didn't promise smooth sailing just a safe harbor

God does not call the equipped. He equips the called.

God does not forget the sinner, He forgets the sin

God does not put anything on us we can't handle.

God does what few men can do – forgets the sins of others.

God doesn't call the qualified, he qualifies the called

God doesn't want your best. He wants your all.

God doesn't want ability, just availability

God grades on the cross, not on the curve.

God has a big eraser!

God has no problems just plans

God hates sin, but does not abandon the sinner

God is love

God is too good to be unkind and to wise to make a mistake.

God is our refuge and strength, a very present help in trouble.

God is the master craftsman. Now let him forge you into a work of art

God is the: universal power supply

God knows what he's doing!

God loves you. Yes even you

God loves you snow much weather you like it or not

God loves you when no one else will.

God makes miracles out of messes and mistakes

God meets our needs in unexpected ways

God moves mountains, but sometimes a shovel full at a time.

God never shuts down

God never tires of hearing us in prayer

God plus one is always the majority

God promised a safe landing... Not smooth sailing

God recycles, he made you from dust

God reworks the world from pieces into peace.

God speaks to those who listen and listens to those who pray

God sweetens outward pain with inward peace.

God wants full custody, not just a weekend visit.

God wants full custody, not weekend visitation.

God wants spiritual fruits, not religious nuts.

God will bring every act to judgment whether good or evil.

God will cause you to be what he calls you to be.

God. Free introductions inside.

God's dream for you is bigger than any dream of your own.

God's forgiveness exists for you as if you were the only person on earth.

God's love inside – come and see

God's not seeking ability- he is seeking availability!

God's part we cannot do. Our part he will not do.

God's re-store. Come in and let your heart be restored.

God's wounds cure, sin's kisses kill.

Gods got your back

God delivers you from the fear of the unknown

God's grace:

God's love for you is real

God's love tough and tender

God's promises are guaranteed for eternity

God's righteousness is available to anyone who asks him

Going the wrong way? God allows U-turns

Good character is like good soup. It's best when homemade.

Good judgment comes from experience, and experience ... Well, that comes from poor judgment.

Good, the more communicated, the more abundant grows.

Gossip is putting two and two together and making five.

Gossip the gospel

Got Jesus?

Got Jesus? It's hell without him

Government making sin legal does not make it right!

Grace is a gift you can share with everyone!

Grace is dispensed because grace has redeemed

Grace: giving us what we do not deserve / mercy: not giving us what we do.

Grass withers and flowers fade, but the word of the lord will stand forever

Great praise often grows out of great pain

Great things the lord hath done

Guest's welcome...members expected!

H

Happiness is an inside job.

Hardening of the heart ages more people than hardening of the arteries.

Has God accepted your friend request?

Hate is not a family value.

Have a nice day...unless you've made other plans.

Have a wonderful and safe mother's day

Have you read my #1 best seller, there will be a test ... God

Have you tried church lately?

Having riches without Christ is dangerous, having Christ without riches is impossible.

He never said it would be easy. He only said we'd never go alone.

He removes the sin and restores the soul

He still speaks to those who listen

He that is born twice will die once

He who kneels before God can stand before anyone

He that is born once will die twice,

He who pays the piper calls the tune.

He who throws dirt loses ground

Heaven is a prepared place for prepared people.

Heaven is for real....so is hell

Heaven will be a treat, hell will be a bad trick!!!!!

Heaven's gold is when the Son is shining in the lives of believers.

Heavenly forecast - reign forever!

Hell ahead. Exit here for heaven

Hell! I thought I'd gotten away with it!

Hell! I thought it didn't matter what you believed as long as you were sincere!

Hell!...I'd forgotten about that!

Hey, God loves you! That's a fact, Jack!

Honk if you love Jesus. Text while driving if you want to meet him.

How good and how pleasant it is for brothers to dwell in unity.

How often do you say, father, thy will be done?

Hypochondria is the only disease i haven't got.

How to take Criticism
Listen to it
Learn from it
Love through it
Live above it

I

I believe we should all pay our tax bill with a smile. I tried — but they wanted cash.

I can't change the Scriptures, but the Scripure can change me.

I don't know how much of God you have, but I know you have all you want!

I don't suffer from insanity. I enjoy every minute of it.

I love you and you and you and you ... God

I have taking a different road, but Jesus is at the end my mine – who is at the end of yours?

I said "no" to drugs, but they just wouldn't listen.

I said yes, which turned out to be the right answer.

I will go anywhere God calls me at any price

I worry whoever thought up the term "quality control" thought if we didn't control it, it would get out of hand.

I've never seen a hearse with a luggage rack

If earth became too comfortable, we would have no desire for heaven.

If not now – When?
If not you – Who?
If not Gospel – What?

If God can deal with eternity, we can handle today!

If God now seems distant, then who strayed?

If God seems far away, guess who moved?

If God used perfect people then nothing would ever get done.

If it ain't broke, don't fix it.

If it pleases you to please the lord...then do as you please

If not today, when?

If we are too busy to pray, we are too busy

If we understand the sin in our hearts

If you are waiting for an earthly kingdom, you will miss a heavenly home.

If you can't be thankful for what you receive, be thankful for what you escape

If you can't stand the heat you better make plans to avoid it

If you can't convince them, confuse them.

If you don't want to reap the fruits of sin stay out of the devil's orchard

If you don't want to reap the fruits of sin stay out of the devil's orchard

If you find it hard to stand for Jesus, try kneeling first

If you had to identify, in one word, the reason why the human race has not achieved, and never will achieve, its full potential, that word would be "meetings".

If you stand for nothing...you'll fall for anything

If you think meek is weak... Try being meek for a week

If you walk with the lord...you'll never be out of step

If you want to stand alone, then don't complain when you fall!

If you want to stand alone, then don't complain when you fall!

If you're far from God in life you'll be far from God in death

If you're not as close to God as you used to be, who moved?

If you're wrinkled with burden... Come in for a faith lift

If you've got time to pray, God's got time to listen.

In the dark? Follow the son

In trying times...don't quit trying

Integrity is who you are when the light is out.

It is unlikely there'll be a reduction in the wages of sin

It isn't our position but our disposition that makes us happy.

It prevents truth decay

It wasn't the apple–it was the pair

It's hard to stumble when you're down on your knees

It's not just to wear the cross...but to bear the cross

It's not too late. Jesus is waiting

It's not what you have in your life,

It's who you have in your life

J

Jesus -- our rock and shelter in the storm

Jesus died for you, live for him

Jesus died, He arose, He is coming again

Jesus is an equal opportunity Savior.

Jesus is an investment that never loses interest

Jesus is life, the rest is details

Jesus is my rock...and my name is on the roll

Jesus is risen and He is Lord

Jesus is the key to eternal life

Jesus is the Lord of life. Is He the Lord of yours?

Jesus is the reason for the season

Jesus is the Shepherd

Jesus lives in the community... He visits the church

Jesus Savior-Son of God

Jesus Savior, helper, friend

Join us today for a faith lift.

Just because your doctor has a name for your condition doesn't mean he knows what it is.

Just when you thought it was safe to ignore God.

K

Keep the faith and share it with others

Keep using my name in vain and i will make rush hour longer ... God

Know God - know peace...no God - no peace

Know Jesus, know peace

L

Laugh a lot, especially at yourself.

Let everything alive praise the lord

Let your heart show you the way.

Let's meet at my house Sunday before the game ... God

Life has many choices, eternity has two. What's yours?

Life is limitless. Time is limited.

Life is shorter than you think.

Life: the ball's in your court after death: it's God's turn

Live for the day, not by the day!

Live life as an exclamation, not an explanation.

Look not behind or ahead, but within.

Lost time is never found

Love does not dominate, it cultivates

Love is a choice, not just a feeling

Love one another

Loved the wedding, invite me to the marriage ... God

Lust is the grandmother of death.

M

Make prayer your 1st choice not your last resort

Making excuses doesn't change the truth.

Man never finds meaning for life until he finds God.

Mary wrapped the first Christmas present.

May all your days have "son shine".

Missions = my involvement seeking sinners in the only name that saves

Morally bankrupt? God offers instant credit.

Morning praise will make your days

Most smiles start with another smile.

Must we die to live?

My favorite bumper stickers says: "All generalizations are false."

My way is the high way ... God

N

Need a lifeguard? Ours walks on water.

Need directions ... God

Never give the devil a ride. He will always want to drive

Never criticize another's sin just because it is different than yours

Never put a question mark where God puts a period.

Never put paperwork before people work.

Never throw dirt...you only lose ground.

No it's not the end of the world, but come to church anyway!

No Jesus, no peace?

No problem is too big to place in God's hands

No two Christians will ever meet for the last time

Not able? - Jesus is!

Nothing will make God love us more or love us less

O

Obey what the Bibles says, not what men say the Bible says.

One day, it'll all make sense.

One expecting to go to heaven should take time to learn the route.

Only God's love will change our world

Only one messiah has an empty grave

Our church is prayer conditioned

Our strength lies in our dependence upon God.

P

Pain is inevitable. Suffering is optional.

Party in hell cancelled due to fire!

Patience is trusting in God's timing.

Peace is not absence of conflict but the ability to cope with it

People are at the heart of God's heart

People don't care how much you know, until they know how much you care.

People don't change because they see the light, but because they feel the heat.

Plant enough seeds, something's going to grow.

Practice an attitude of gratitude...pray!

Practice random acts of kindness.

Pray until something happens (push).

Prayer is an open line to heaven

Prayer need not be eloquent, only sincere

Prayer often begins with a confession of sin

Prayer should be your first resource, not your last.

Prayer...the next best thing to being there

Preach the gospel at all times. Use words if necessary.

Prevent truth decay. Brush up on your Bible

Pro-choice: that's a lie! Babies do not choose to die!

Provide things honest in the sight of all men.

Put fears to rest, by faith in Jesus

Put your trust in the lord

R

Remember the banana. When it got separated from the bunch, it got peeled.

Remember what's at the center of sin, "I" am.

Repent now! Avoid the rush on judgment day!

Reputation is what people think about you. Character is what people know you are

Rule #1... God is in control. Rule #2... See rule #1.

S

Salvation is received, not achieved

Salvation: free to us, costly to God

Satan subtracts and divides. God multiplies and multiplies

Satan wears camouflage

Satan will accept your service on a part-time basis, but God will not.

Seven days without prayer makes one weak

Shall we interpret the Bible by our experiences or do we interpret our experience by the Bible?

Shouldn't complain when they get splinters.

Show God's love. Share God's love. Be God's love.

Show love in words and deeds

Sign broken...come inside for message

Simplify meditation. Sit down and shut up!

Sin burn is prevented by son screen.

Sin is a very short word beginning a very long sentence.

Sin is the disease. Jesus is the cure. Get the prescription

Sin sees the bait, but is blind to the hook.

Sin will always keep you longer than you want to stay

Sin will always take you farther than you want to go

Sin will take you further than you want to go and cost you more than you want to pay

Sin will take you further than you want to go and keep you longer than you want to stay!!!

Sin would be less attractive if the wages were paid immediately

Sin: You may get by with it but you will never get away with it!

Sin: it seemed like a good idea at the time

Sincerity is no substitute for the truth, nor guarantee of it.

Sinners have a future. What's yours?

Slow down and let God love you like never before

Smile often. If your face hurts, then you are out of shape.

Smile! It increases your face value.

So you think its hot now

Some answers just cannot be found on google - try the Bible ... God

Some people talk about finding God as if he could get lost.

Sunrise, a gift from God

Soul food served here

Spread the gospel not the gossip

Start your day with God. It ends better.

Sticks and stones may break a bone, but words can break a heart.

Stop, drop & roll won't work in hell.

Stop, drop and roll does not work in hell.

T

T.G.I.F....thank God I'm forgiven

Tell the kids I love them ... God

Thankfulness is the soul that joy thrives in

Thanks be to God for his unspeakable gift

That "love thy neighbor' thing, I meant it ... God

That that is, is, that that is not, is not. [Try understanding that without the commas set]

That's the silliest thing I ever assimilated

The atheist greatest hope is there is no life after death

The best cleanser ever created was the blood of Christ!

The best gift anyone can receive is Jesus

The best is yet to be.

The less you hear me now. The more you will need Me later.

The best remedy for discontent is to count our blessings.

The best room is room for improvement.

The best things in life, are not physical things

The best vitamin for a Christian is b1

The best way to remember people is in prayer

The Bible is bread for daily use, not cake for special occasions.

The deep peace of God

The devil may be stoking the fire, but God has his hand on the thermostat.

The devil's trick is no treat

The greatest freedom of all …is freedom from sin!

The greatest of evils is our indifference towards evil!

The largest room in the world is the room for improvement.

The light of the world knows no power failure

The lord blesses his people with peace

The lord gave us commandments. He didn't mention amendments.

The lord is my helper, I will not be afraid

The most terrible pain is a troubled conscience

The next time you think you're perfect try walking on water!

The only power you have is the word 'no'.

The only preparation for tomorrow is the proper use of today

The person who hasn't time to read the Bible hasn't time to go to heaven.

The road to hell is paved with good intentions.

The road to success is always under construction.

The sin we try to cover up will eventually bring us down

The speed you are making is not as important as the direction headed.

The transition from time to eternity is instantaneous

The wages of sin are death. Quit before payday.

The wages of sin is death. Repent before payday

There are 2 types of people, sinners who think they are righteous and the righteous who know they are sinners

There are only two masters – who do you serve?

There are two things you need to know...1.there is a God. 2. You are not him!

There is a way to stay out of hell, but no way to get out.

There is always light at the end of the tunnel - if there isn't, it's not a tunnel...

There is no moral difference between legal and illegal gambling.

There is no strength in numbers when you are wrong

There will be no atheists in hell

There's more hope for murderers than the self-righteous

Things you can count on: death and taxes. Are you ready for both?

Those who go against the grain of God's laws

Three things necessary for a Christian: determination, direction and God

Three ways the devil wins: excuses, indifference, and procrastination

Tithe if you love Jesus! Anyone can honk!

To arrive at the right destination, you must travel the right road.

To avoid sin's tragedy...learn Satan's strategy

To be almost saved is to be totally lost

To belittle is to be little

To create something you love

To know the strength of the anchor... You need to feel the storm

To love God is to obey God

To stop reaping bad fruits, stay out of Satan's orchard.

Today is the first day of the rest of your life

Today's to do list...thank Jesus

Together in Christ

Tomorrows forecast, God reigns and the son shines

Triumph is just umph added to try!

Trouble looks back, worry looks ahead, faith looks up

Troubles are often the tools by which God fashions us for better things.

Truth crushed to the ground will rise again

Truth is always the strongest argument

Try Jesus. If you don't like him, the devil will always take you back.

Turn a frown upside down.

Turn or burn

Turn right and go straight.

Turn your life over to God and he will turn over your life

Two choices on the shelf...live for God or live for self.

U

Ultimate reality: God is, God loves, God can be found

Under the same management for 2000 years

Uninspired by Jesus? Bet you really haven't met him.

Unless the lord builds the house, they labor in vain who build.

Usually reveals a life that isn't

Virtue is never more obvious that doing right when no one is looking

W

Wal-Mart is not the only saving place

We also deal with fire and rescue!

We are not dairy queen...but we have great Sundays

We are the caregivers, and God is the curegiver.

We can only appreciate grace

We don't change the message...the message changes us

We have a great prophet-sharing plan. Details inside.

We need sin control-not gun control

We need to talk ... God

We wait for the world to regenerate while God waits for us to repent!

Welcome to our CH   CH...What's missing - UR

What can we expect from heaven?

What does it take for God to get our attention?

What God sends is better than what we ask for.

What on earth are you doing for heaven's sake?

What part of "thou shalt not" did you not understand ... God

What part of "thou shalt not" don't you understand?

What should not be heard by little ears should not be said by big mouths.

What will he say to you – enter my kingdom or depart from me

What would you do today if you knew Christ was coming tomorrow?

When faithfulness is most difficult, it is most necessary.

When God forgives,

When God saw you it was love at first sight

When I was a boy i was told that anybody could become president. I'm beginning to believe it.

When in doubt, don't!

When Jesus comes into a life, he changes everything

When life gives you lemons, make lemonade!

When one door shuts, another opens.

When praying, don't give God instructions. Just report for duty.

When Satan knocks, say, "Jesus, would you get that?"

When the devil reminds you of your past, remind him of his future.

When the going gets tough, the tough get going.

When trouble grows, your character shows

When you are in deep water, trust the one who walked on it.

When you kill time, you murder success.

When you think you're perfect, try walking on water.

When you were born the world rejoiced. Live so when you die you will rejoice.

When you were born, you cried and the world rejoiced. Live your life so that when you die, the world cries and you rejoice

When your time has come you will know of every missed opportunity. Do you really want to gamble heaven and hell?

Where will you be seated in eternity...smoking or non-smoking?

Whoever believes in the son has eternal life

Why can't you play cards on a small boat? Because someone is always sitting on the deck.

Why worry when you can pray

Will the road you are on get you to my place?

Will the road you're on get to my place ... God?

Will your eternal home be smoking or non-smoking?

Worried about truth decay? Try brushing up on your Bible.

Worry is a merry-go-round...except it rides you

Worry is interest paid on trouble before it is due.

Worship is a verb!

World's Philosophy: Get all you can, can all you get, then sell the can.

Wrong is always wrong, even if everyone does it.

Y

You can lead a horse to water, but you can't make it drink.

You don't have to be brain-dead to live for Jesus, but when you are, you'll be glad you did

You think it's hot here ... God

You think life is full of surprises? Wait till you die!

Your hereafter depends upon what you are after here!

Share your quotes or thoughts with me for future editions.

Alton.loveless@prodigy.net

Church Marquee Signs

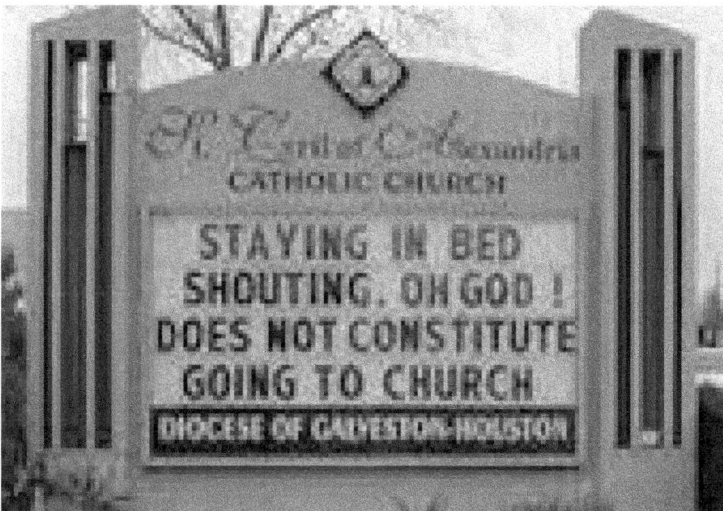

SPRINGFIELD
BIBLE CHURCH

KEEP ON TEXTING
WHILE DRIVING TO
MEET JESUS SOONER.

BIBLE CLASSES, 9:30am WORSHIP, 10:30am

869-0463
2145 East Grand

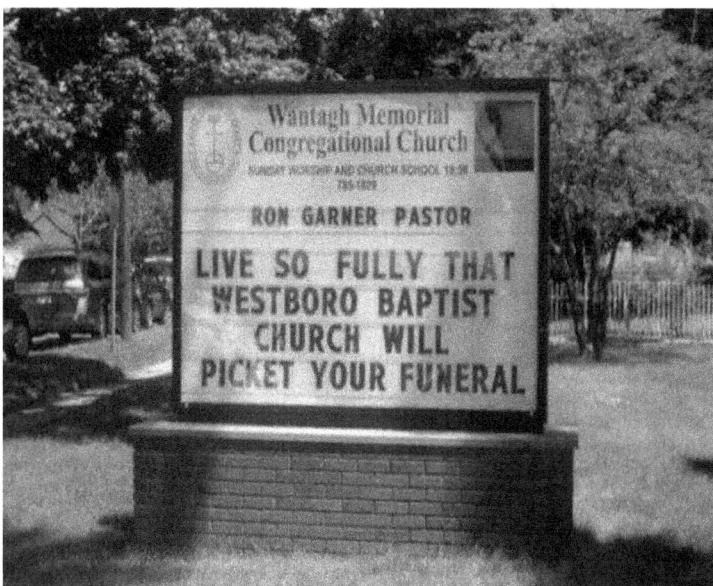

Wantagh Memorial
Congregational Church
SUNDAY WORSHIP AND CHURCH SCHOOL 10:30

RON GARNER PASTOR

LIVE SO FULLY THAT
WESTBORO BAPTIST
CHURCH WILL
PICKET YOUR FUNERAL

www.StrangePersons.com

Tuckaseege
BAPTIST CHURCH

GOD'S
LAST NAME
IS NOT
DAMN

FEEL YOU'RE BEING TAKEN
FOR GRANTED
IMAGINE HOW GOD FEELS

CANAL FULTON
BAPTIST CHURCH

PEACE IN A WORLD
IN TURMOIL
JESUS IS THE
ANSWER
ISAIAH 26:3

Hope Community Church

SUNDAY WORSHIP
SERVICE-10:00AM
BE THANKFUL YOU
DON'T GET WHAT
YOU DESERVE

BRAGGTOWN
BAPTIST CHURCH
SUNDAY SCHOOL 9:30 WORSHIP 10:45 WED. 6:30 PM

MAN'S WAY LEADS TO A
HOPELESS END! GOD'S WAY
LEADS TO A ENDLESS HOPE!

CENTRAL
BAPTIST

THINK ITS
HOT HERE
HELL IS EVEN HOTTER

IMMANUEL BAPTIST CHURCH

WORSHIP 11:00AM

PROBLEMS ARE ONLY OPPORTUNITIES IN WORK CLOTHES

SUNDAY SCHOOL 9:45AM

Calvary Baptist Temple

2420 LaPorte Ave
Ft. Collins, CO 80521

484.2477/ 416.0143

PASTORS
DR. WILLIAM (BILLY) SUTTON
REV. PARK SUTTON
WWW.CALVARYBAPTISTTEMPLE.NET

A FATHER KNOWS BEST WHEN HE KNOWS JESUS

SOUTH BROOKLEY UNITED METHODIST CHURCH

PASTOR   SUN SCHOOL   WORSHIP
REV. DOUG JOLLY   9:45AM   11:00AM

GOD HAS GIVEN US SOMETHING THAT BOEING CAN NEVER TAKE AWAY

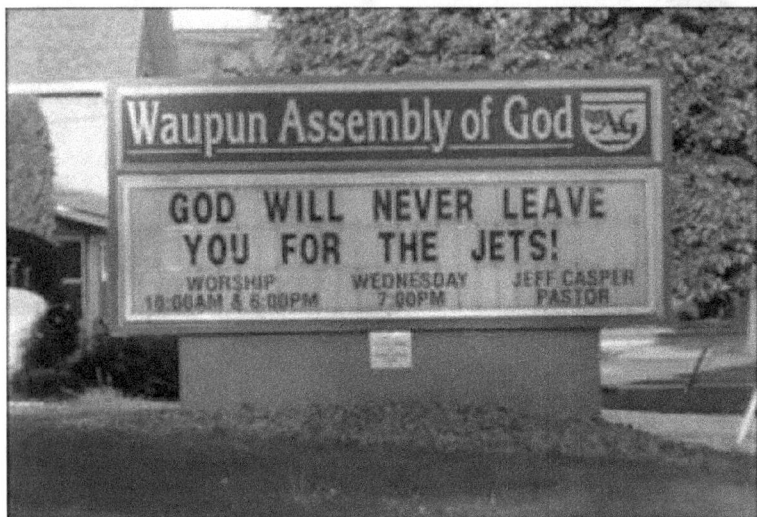

Waupun Assembly of God

GOD WILL NEVER LEAVE YOU FOR THE JETS!

WORSHIP   WEDNESDAY   JEFF CASPER
10:00AM & 6:00PM   7:00PM   PASTOR

FIRST BAPTIST
CHURCH OF MAYVIEW

WE'RE ALL IN THIS TOGETHER.
WE NEED EACH OTHER.
COMMUNITY IS IMPORTANT.
EVEN JESUS HAD DISCIPLES.

BETHLEHEM TEMPLE
APOSTOLIC FAITH CHURCH

Bishop LARRY J. COPELAND, Pastor
SUNDAY SCHOOL 9:45AM • MORNING WORSHIP 11:30AM • EVANGELISTICAL SERVICE 6:00PM
BIBLE STUDY WED 7:30PM • PRAYER SERVICE FRI 7:30PM

WHATS MISSING IN CH CH -UR

LEDGE ROCK
BAPTIST CHURCH
SUNDAY SCHOOL 9:45AM WORSHIP 11:00AM BIBLE STUDY WEDNESDAY 7:30PM
Pastor NATHANIEL R. FULLER
THE LORD IS MY SHEPARD

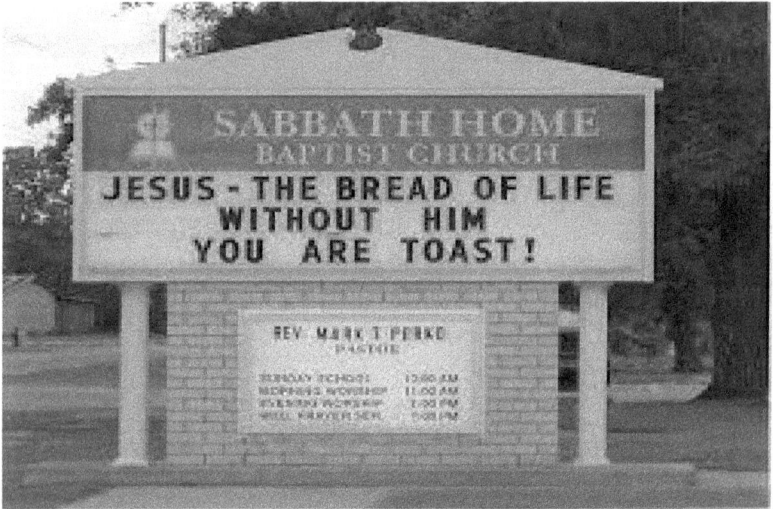

SABBATH HOME
BAPTIST CHURCH

JESUS - THE BREAD OF LIFE
WITHOUT HIM
YOU ARE TOAST!

REV. MARK T. PERKO
PASTOR

UNITY CHURCH of DALLAS
A CENTER FOR PRACTICAL CHRISTIANITY

EVERYTHING YOU EVER
WANTED TO KNOW
ABOUT LABYRINTHS
MONDAY 7:00
JOHN LIPINSKI
UNITYDALLAS.ORG

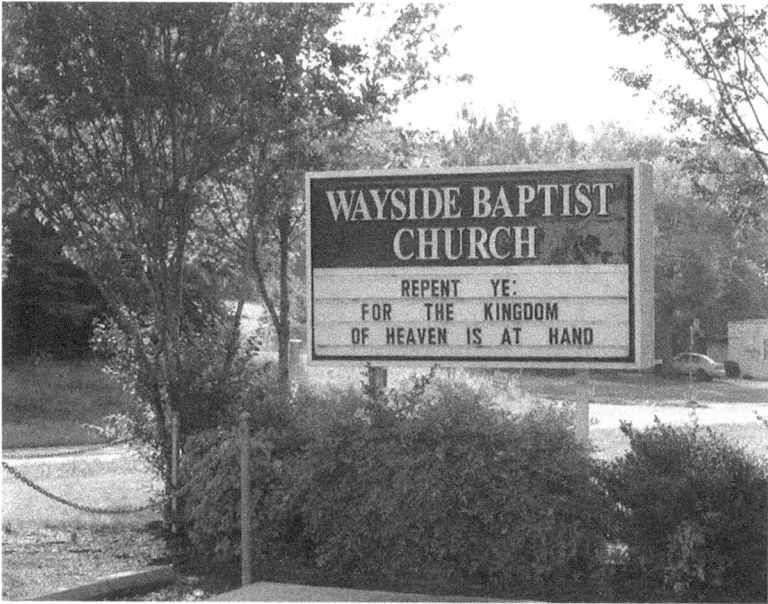

WAYSIDE BAPTIST CHURCH

REPENT YE:
FOR THE KINGDOM
OF HEAVEN IS AT HAND

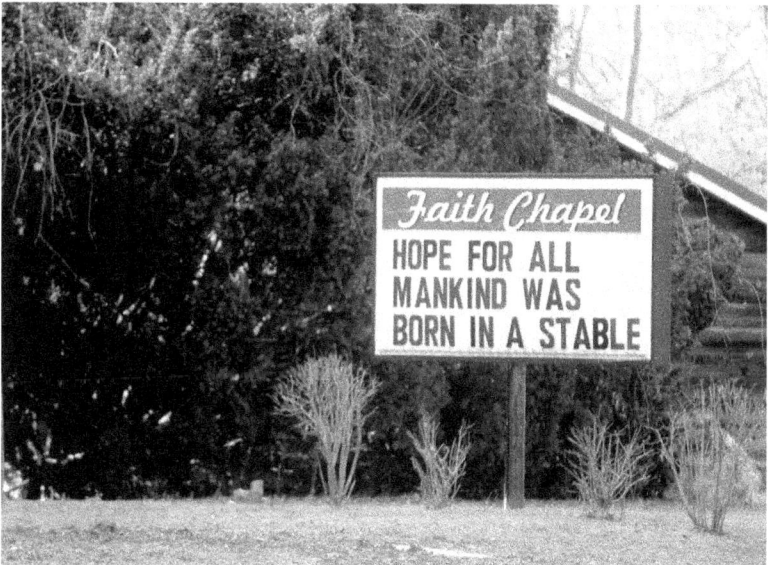

Faith Chapel

HOPE FOR ALL
MANKIND WAS
BORN IN A STABLE

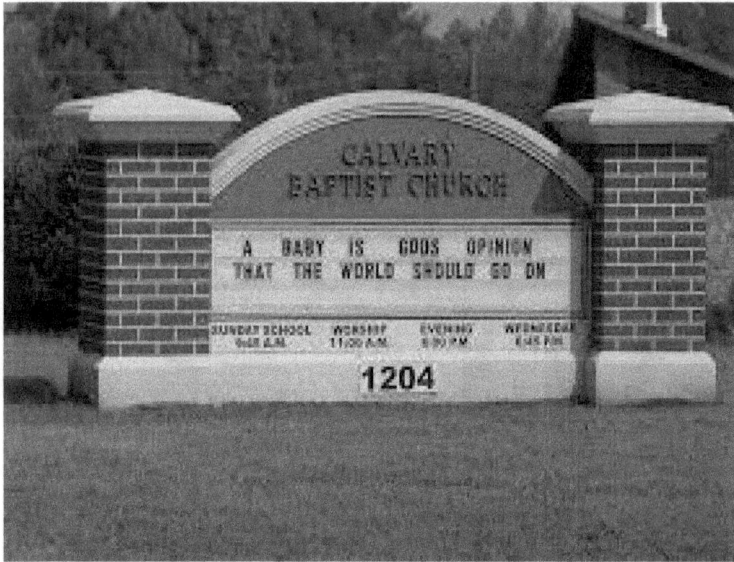

Ivyland New Church

WE BELIEVE
ALL RELIGIONS LEAD
TO HEAVEN

Worship Sunday 10AM

MONTESSORI
Preschool + K
(215) 431-4243

Fellowship
FREE WILL BAPTIST CHURCH

WELCOME
TO
FELLOWSHIP

1228 WEST VILLA MARIA
Bible Study 9:45 – Morning Worship 10:45
Sunday Night 6:00 – Wednesday 6:30
DOUG DICKEY, PASTOR

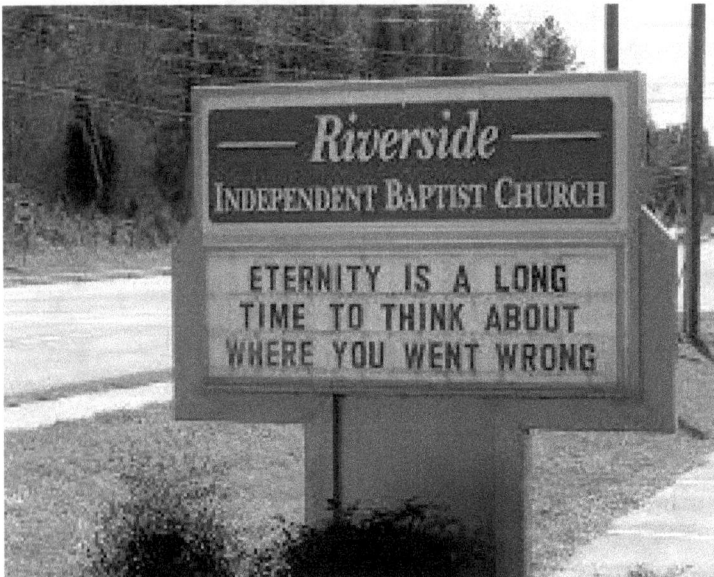

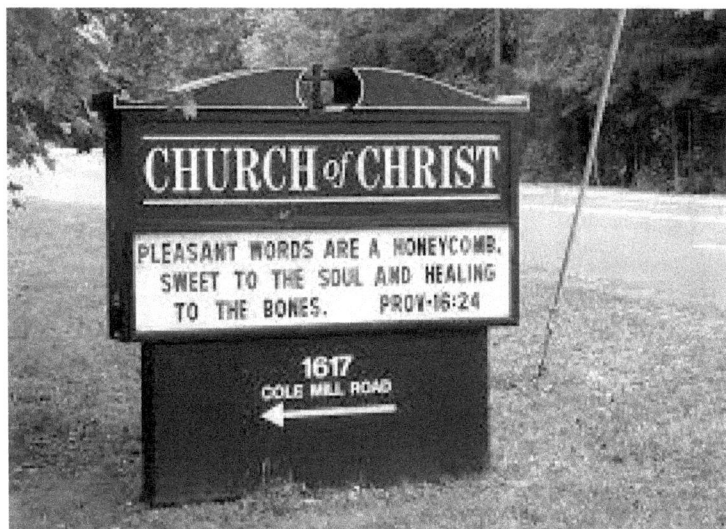

CHURCH of CHRIST

PLEASANT WORDS ARE A HONEYCOMB,
SWEET TO THE SOUL AND HEALING
TO THE BONES.   PROV-16:24

1617
COLE MILL ROAD

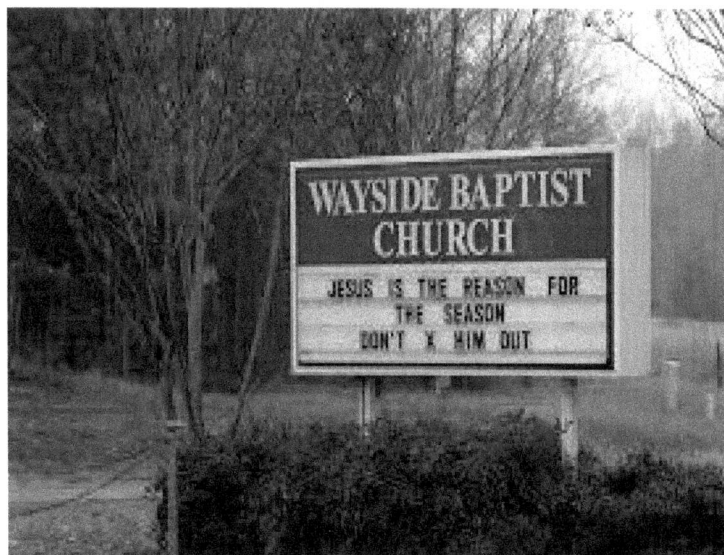

WAYSIDE BAPTIST
CHURCH

JESUS IS THE REASON FOR
THE SEASON
DON'T X HIM OUT

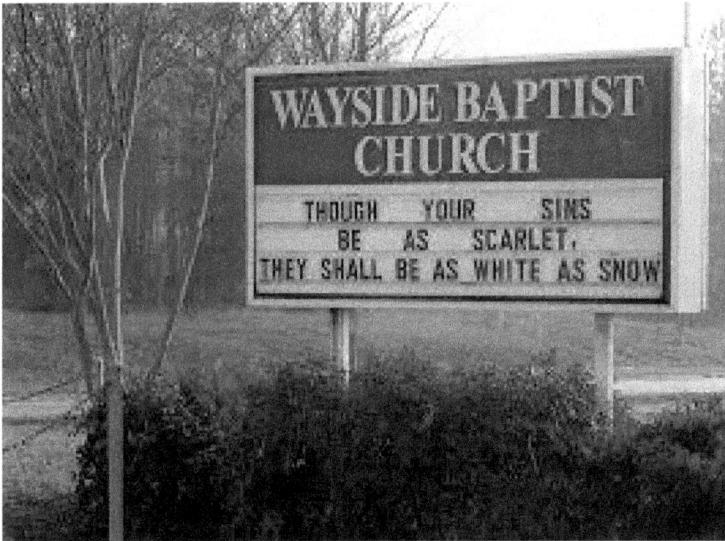

WAYSIDE BAPTIST CHURCH

THOUGH YOUR SINS BE AS SCARLET, THEY SHALL BE AS WHITE AS SNOW

GETHSEMANE MISSIONARY BAPTIST CHURCH

PRAY WORSHIP AND LIVE

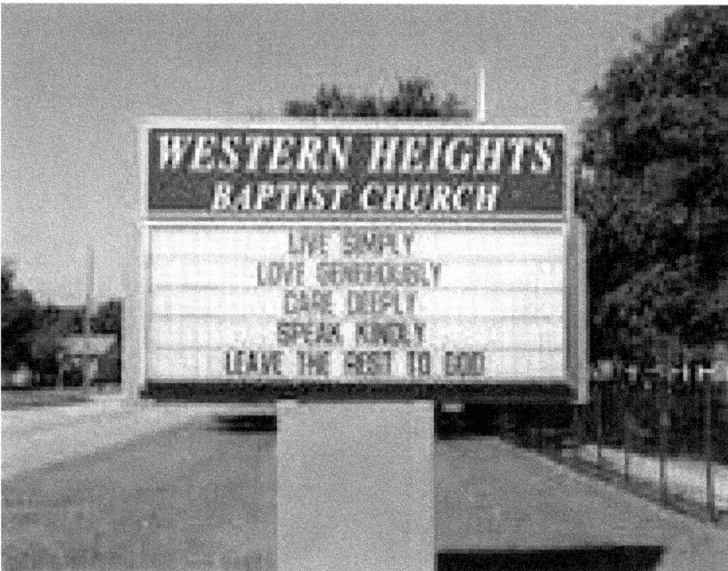

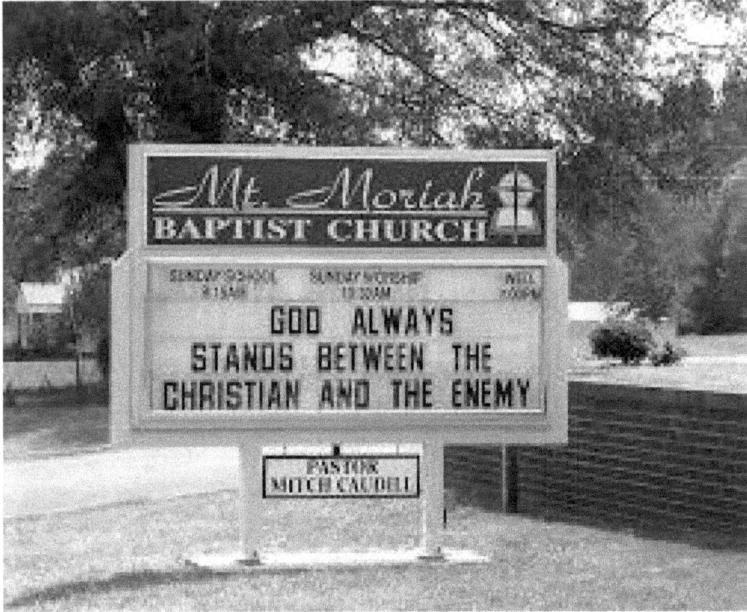

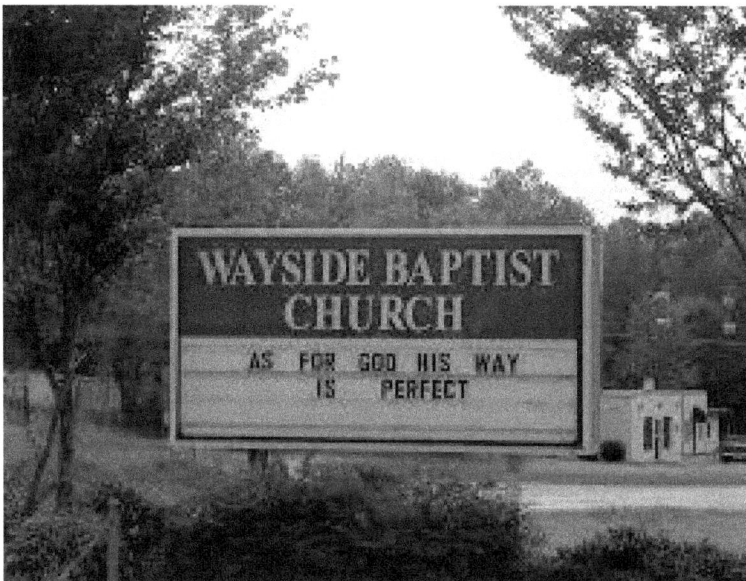

WAYSIDE BAPTIST CHURCH

AS FOR GOD HIS WAY IS PERFECT

NORTHGATE PRESBYTERIAN CHURCH

David Keck : Pastor

MAKE A JOYFUL NOISE

BREA CONGREGATIONAL
UNITED CHURCH OF CHRIST
THOU SHALT NOT
USE DRONES
TO KILL
WORSHIP SUN 10AM

TRUE LIGHT KOREAN CHURCH
참빛한인교회
Tel: 714-741-9636, 495-0055

Abundant Life
LUTHERAN CHURCH
OPEN ARMS CHILD CARE

HAPPY
FIRST BIRTHDAY
OPEN ARMS

3320   Rev. Wally Shiffett, Pastor

Mentor Community Church of God

WORSHIP 10:30 AM
PASTOR ED HAGER

AMERICA'S HERITAGE
IS CHRISTIANITY

Cape Fear Baptist Church

INDEPENDENT & FUNDAMENTAL

Sunday School 10 AM – Sunday Worship 11 AM & 6 PM – Wed. Worship 7 PM

WHY IS THE MOST
RESTFUL DAY OF
THE WEEK –
PASTOR: DAVID BRADDY – 910-350-8224

HEAVEN
IS NO TRICK
HELL
IS NO TREAT

MANTEO
BAPTIST CHURCH

GOD IS LIKE
SCOTCH TAPE
YOU CAN'T SEE HIM
BUT YOU KNOW HE'S THERE

CROSSROADS
CHURCH OF CHRIST

DUST ON YOUR BIBLE
COULD LEAD TO
DIRT IN YOUR LIFE

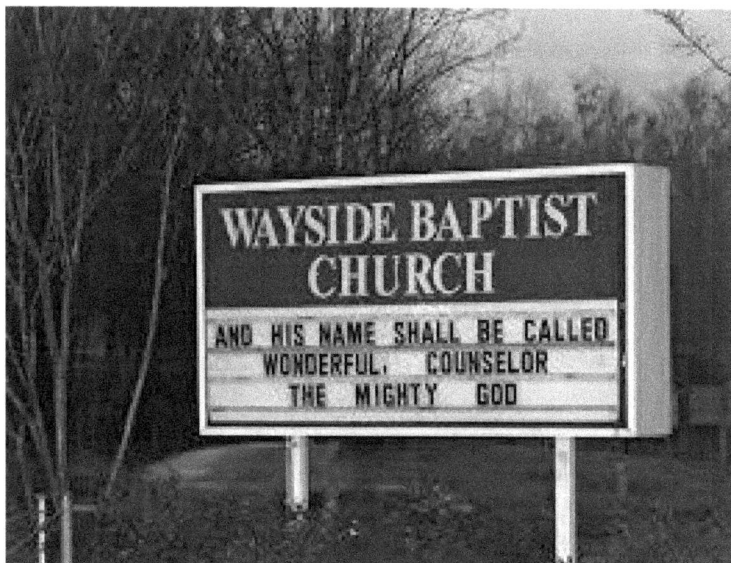

WAYSIDE BAPTIST CHURCH

AND HIS NAME SHALL BE CALLED
WONDERFUL, COUNSELOR
THE MIGHTY GOD

Cornerstone
Assembly of God

GOD'S WORD IS THE
COMPASS THAT KEEPS
US ON COURSE

CHURCH of CHRIST

A WORD APTLY SPOKEN IS LIKE
APPLES OF GOLD IN SETTINGS
OF SILVER. PROV-25:11

1617
COLE MILL ROAD

FIRST
BAPTIST
CHURCH

SUNDAY SERVICES
WORSHIP
9:00AM
10:30AM
BIBLE STUDY
9:00AM
10:30AM

www.says-it.com/churchsigns/

PRAY FOR OUR
PRESIDENT

TO BE REPLACED

Unitarian Universalist Congregation

To dream of the person you would like to be is to waste the person you are.
www.uuchnc.org

Services and Religious Educatio
10:30 Sundays

644-0567

House of Prayer

EAT THE DEVILS CORN
YOU WILL
CHOKE ON HIS COB

REMEMBER
SATAN WAS THE FIRST
TO DEMAND EQUAL RIGHTS

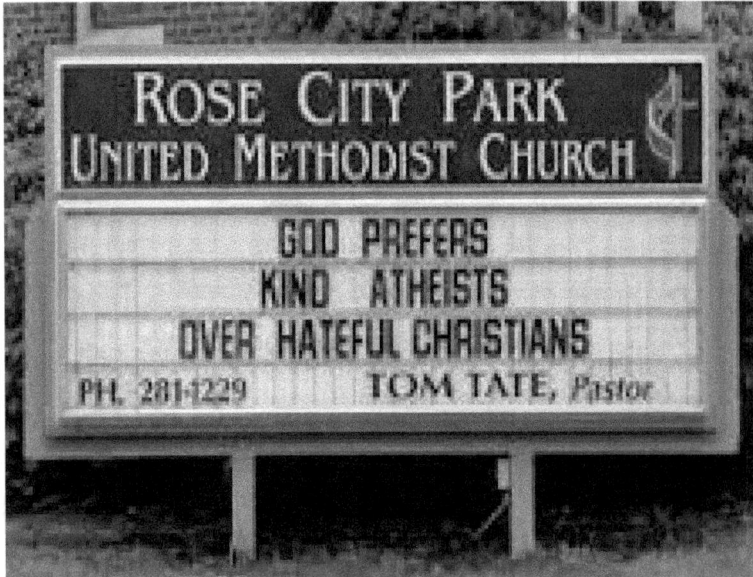

ROSE CITY PARK
UNITED METHODIST CHURCH

GOD PREFERS
KIND ATHEISTS
OVER HATEFUL CHRISTIANS

PH. 281-1229   TOM TATE, *Pastor*

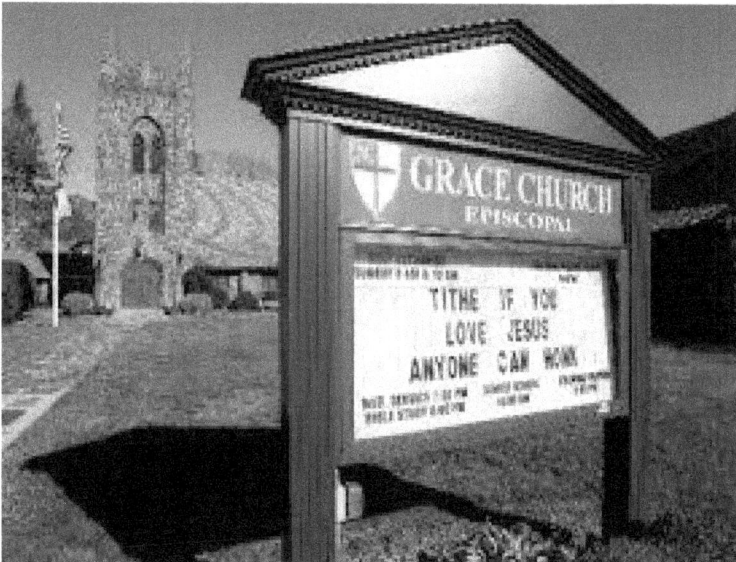

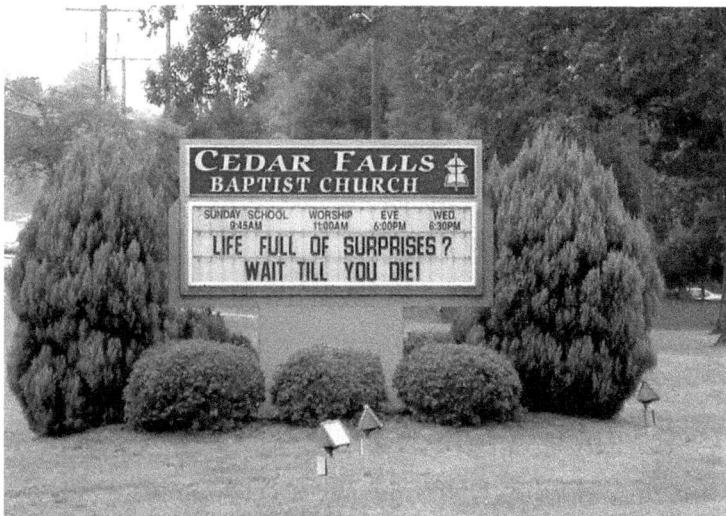

CEDAR FALLS
BAPTIST CHURCH

| SUNDAY SCHOOL | WORSHIP | EVE | WED. |
| 9:45AM | 11:00AM | 6:00PM | 6:30PM |

LIFE FULL OF SURPRISES?
WAIT TILL YOU DIE!

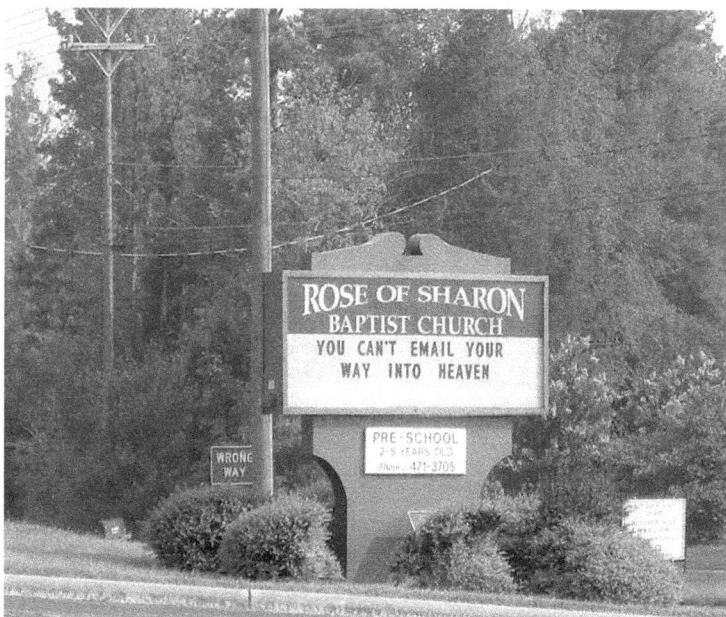

ROSE OF SHARON
BAPTIST CHURCH
YOU CAN'T EMAIL YOUR
WAY INTO HEAVEN

PRE-SCHOOL
2-5 YEARS OLD
Phone 471-3705

WRONG
WAY

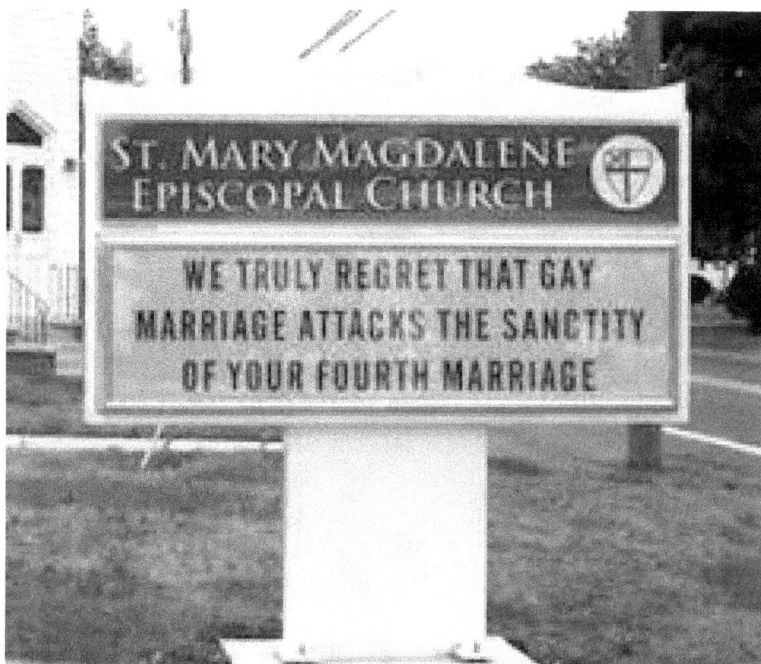

GOD CAN TAKE
THE ORDINARY AND
MAKE IT
EXTRAORDINARY

THREE FORKS
BAPTIST
CHURCH

MOUNT OLIVE
A.M.E. ZION CHURCH

COMMAND YOUR
MORNING

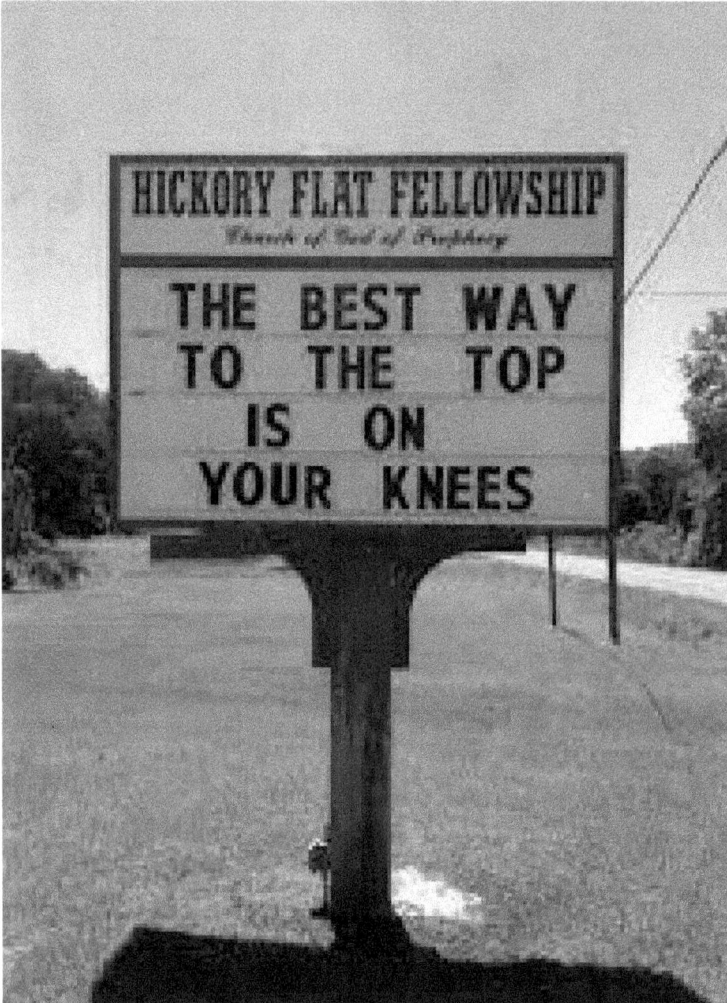

HICKORY FLAT FELLOWSHIP
Church of God of Prophecy

THE BEST WAY
TO THE TOP
IS ON
YOUR KNEES

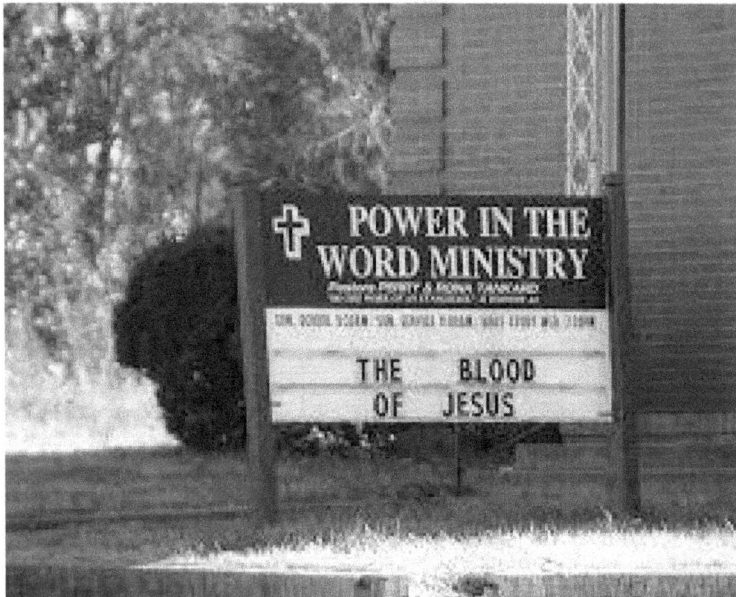

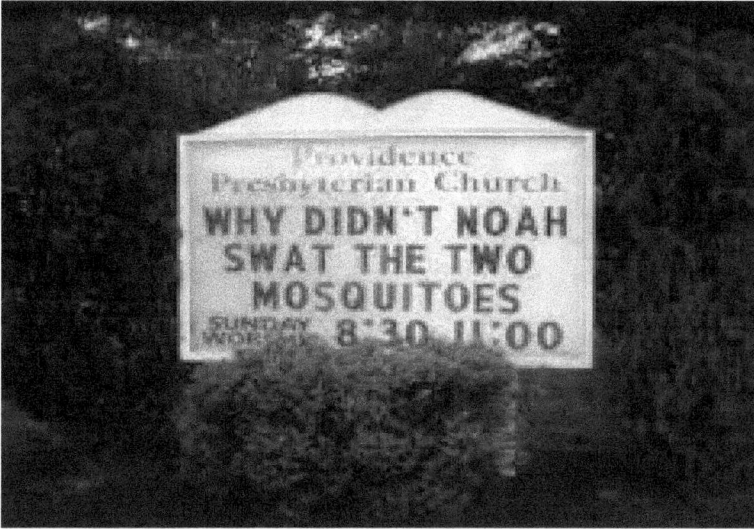

Providence
Presbyterian Church
WHY DIDN'T NOAH
SWAT THE TWO
MOSQUITOES
SUNDAY
WORSHIP 8:30 11:00

MT. CARMEL
UNITED METHODIST CHURCH

A NATION IS NEVER MORE THAN
ONE GENERATION AWAY FROM ATHEISM.
WHAT WILL BE OUR LEGACY?

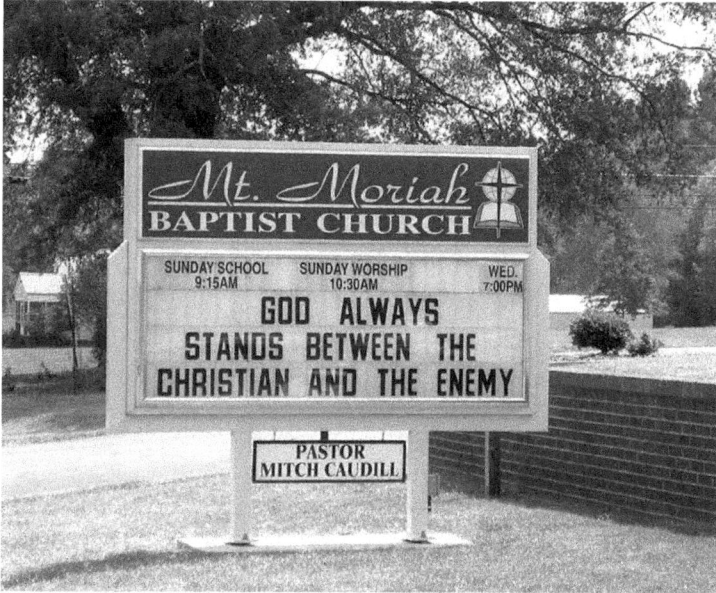

Mt. Moriah
BAPTIST CHURCH

| SUNDAY SCHOOL 9:15AM | SUNDAY WORSHIP 10:30AM | WED. 7:00PM |

GOD ALWAYS STANDS BETWEEN THE CHRISTIAN AND THE ENEMY

PASTOR MITCH CAUDILL

MANY WHO SEEK GOD AT THE ELEVENTH HOUR DIE AT 10:30

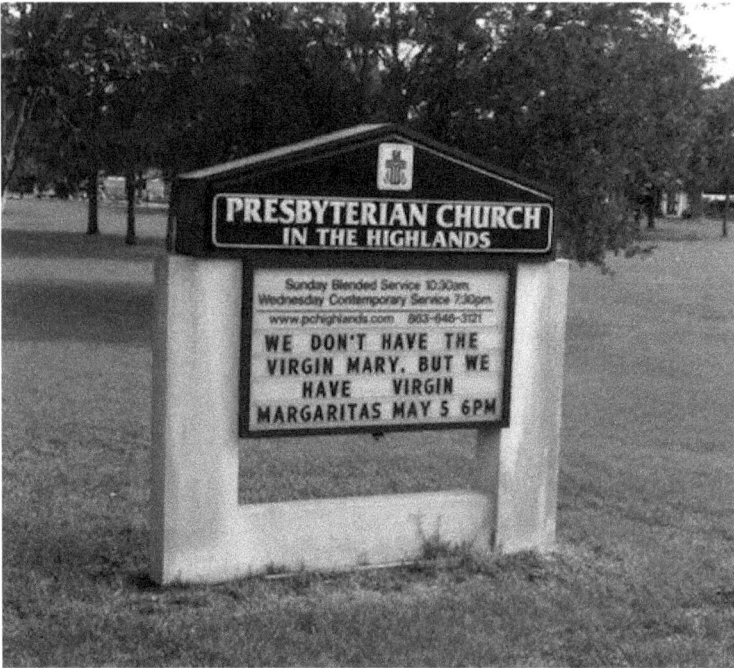

PRESBYTERIAN CHURCH
IN THE HIGHLANDS

Sunday Blended Service 10:30am
Wednesday Contemporary Service 7:30pm
www.pchighlands.com   863-646-3121
WE DON'T HAVE THE
VIRGIN MARY, BUT WE
HAVE   VIRGIN
MARGARITAS MAY 5 6PM

First Baptist Church
of Morrisville

WISDOM IS   FALL
REFINED   CARNIVAL
STUPIDITY   10 31 6PM

REV.
MYRON YANDLE
Entrance at
209 Church St.

Funny Tombstone Sayings

Sir John Strange;
Here lies an honest lawyer,
And that is Strange.
-- Tombstone in England

I was somebody.
Who, is no business Of yours.
-- Vermont tombstone

Here lies Lester Moore;
Four slugs from a .44;
No Les No More.
-- Tombstone Arizona

John Brown is filling his last cavity.
-- Dentist's Tombstone

He was young
He was fair
But the Injuns
Raised his hair
-- Arizona Tombstone

I told you that I was sick!
-- Georgia Cemetery

Here lies the body of Jonathan Blake;
Stepped on the gas instead of the brake.
-- Pennsylvania Tombstone

Bill Blake
Was hanged by mistake.
-- Colorado Tombstone

Remember man, as you walk by,
As you are now, so once was I,
As I am now, so shall you be,
Remember this and follow me.
-- Tombstone in England
To follow you I'll not consent,
Until I know which way you went.
-- Written on the tombstone in reply to one above

Here lays Butch.
We planted him raw.
He was quick on the trigger
But slow on the draw.
-- Arizona Tombstone

The children of Israel wanted bread,
And the Lord sent them manna,
Old clerk Wallace wanted a wife,
And the Devil sent him Anna.
-- England Tombstone

Under the sod and under the trees,
Lies the body of Jonathan Pease.
He is not here, there's only the pod;
Pease shelled out and went to God.
-- Massachusetts Tombstone

Here lies the body of Arkansas Jim.
We made the mistake, but the jokes on him.
-- Kansas Tombstone

Gone away, Owin' more
than he could pay.
-- England

To save your world you asked this man to die:
Would this man, could he see you now, ask why?
-- Unknown Soldier

She always said her feet were killing her, but nobody
believed her.
-- Virginia tombstone

Here lies the body of
Thomas Kemp.
Who lived by wool
and died by hemp.
-- Ireland Tombstone

For God And His Country He Raised Our Flag In Battle And
Showed A Measure Of His Pride At A Place Called "Iwo
Jima" Where Courage Never Died
-- A soldiers memorial

Here lies the body
Of Margaret Bent
She kicked up her heels
And away she went
-- England Tombstone

If I should die, think only this of me:
That there's some corner of a foreign
field that is forever England
-- Tombstone in England

He got a fish-bone in his throat
and then he sang an angel note.
-- New York Tombstone

Here lies the body of our Anna
Done to death by a banana
It wasn't the fruit that laid her low
But the skin of the thing that made her go.
-- Unknown Tombstone

Captain Thomas Coffin
Died 1842, age 50 years.
He's done a-catching cod
And gone to meet his God.
-- A fisherman's tombstone

Mary Weary, Housewife
Dere Friends I am going
Where washing ain't done
Or cooking or sewing:

Don't mourn for me now
Or weep for me never:
For I go to do nothing
Forever and ever!
-- House wife tombstone

Here lies the father of 29.
He would have had more
But he didn't have time.
-- Georgia Tombstone

Here lies Johnny Yeast
Pardon me For not rising.
-- New Mexico tombstone

Here beneath this stone we lie
Back to back my wife and I
And when the angels trump shall trill
If she gets up then I'll lie still!
--Scotland Tombstone

Here lies
an Atheist
All dressed up
And no place to go.
-- Maryland Tombstone

Beneath this stone a lump of clay
Lies Uncle Peter Dan'els
Who early in the month of May
Took off his winter flannels.
-- Scotland Tombstone

Reader, I've left this world, in which
I had a world to do;
Sweating and fretting to get rich:
Just such a fool as you.
-- Carolina Tombstone

Once I wasn't
Then I was
Now I ain't again.
-- Ohio Tombstone

www.ingramcontent.com/pod-product-compliance
Lightning Source LLC
Chambersburg PA
CBHW050537280326
41933CB00011B/1620